Six Sessions
PARTICIPANT'S GUIDE

Believing in God but Living as If He Doesn't Exist

theChris†ianatheist

CRAIG

GROESCHEL

with Christine M. Anderson

ZONDERVAN®

ZONDERVAN.com/
AUTHORTRACKER
follow your favorite authors

ZONDERVAN

The Christian Atheist Participant's Guide
Copyright © 2011 by Craig Groeschel

Requests for information should be addressed to:
Zondervan, *Grand Rapids, Michigan 49530*

ISBN 978-0-310-32975-6

Published in association with Winters, King & Associates, Inc.

Cover design: Design Works Group / Tim Green
Interior design: Matthew Van Zomeren

Printed in the United States of America

15 16 /DCI/ 25 24 23 22 21 20 19 18 17 16 15 14 13 12 11 10

Believing in God but Living as If He Doesn't Exist

theChris✝ianatheist

Also by Craig Groeschel

Weird: Because Normal Isn't Working

The Christian Atheist: Believing in God but Living as If He Doesn't Exist

It: How Churches and Leaders Can Get It and Keep It

What Is God Really Like? (general editor)

Chazown: A Different Way to See Your Life

Going All the Way: Preparing for a Marriage That Goes the Distance

Confessions of a Pastor: Adventures in Dropping the Pose

Contents

How to Use This Guide

Group Size

The Christian Atheist video curriculum is designed to be experienced in a group setting such as a Bible study, Sunday school class, or any small group gathering. To ensure everyone has enough time to participate in discussions, it is recommended that large groups break up into smaller groups of four to six people each.

Materials Needed

Each participant should have his or her own Participant's Guide, which includes video outline notes, directions for activities, and discussion questions, as well as a reading plan and personal studies to deepen learning between sessions. Although the course can be fully experienced with just the video and Participant's Guide, participants are also encouraged to have a copy of *The Christian Atheist* book. Reading the book alongside the video curriculum provides even deeper insights that make the journey richer and more meaningful.

Timing

The time notations — for example (17 minutes) — indicate the *actual* time of DVD segments and the *suggested* times for each activity or discussion. For example:

Individual Activity **Three Things to Remember** (3 Minutes)

Adhering to the suggested times will enable you to complete each session in one hour. If you have additional time, you may wish to allow more time for discussion and activities.

Facilitation

Each group should appoint a facilitator who is responsible for starting the video and for keeping track of time during discussions and activities. Facilitators may also read questions aloud and monitor discussions, prompting participants to respond and assuring that everyone has the opportunity to participate.

Between-Sessions Personal Study

Maximize the impact of the course with additional study between group sessions. Setting aside about an hour for personal study will enable you to complete the book and between-session studies by the end of the course. For each session, you may wish to complete the personal study all in one sitting or to spread it out over a few days.

When You Believe in God but Don't Really Know Him

THEISM
[**thee**-iz-*uh*m]
belief in the existence of God

ATHEISM
[**ey**-thee-iz-*uh*m]
disbelief in the existence of God

PRACTICAL ATHEISM
[**prak**-ti-k*uh*l **ey**-thee-iz-*uh*m]
acting with apathy, disregard, or lack of interest toward belief in God

CHRISTIAN
[**kris**-ch*uh*n]
one who professes belief in the teachings of Christ

CHRISTIAN ATHEISM
[**kris**-ch*uh*n **ey**-thee-iz-*uh*m]
believing in Christ but living as if he doesn't exist

Video — When You Believe in God but Don't Really Know Him
(18 Minutes)

Play the video segment for session 1. As you watch, use the outline below to follow along or to take notes on anything that stands out to you.

Notes

So many people believe in God but they do not know him (Titus 1:16).

Three levels of knowing God

- Level 1: *I believe in God, but I don't know him.*

- Level 2: *I believe in God, but I don't know him well.*

     Galatians 4:8 – 9

- Level 3: *I believe in God, know him intimately, and serve him wholeheartedly.*

     Example: David is described as a man after God's own heart (1 Samuel 13:14).

     Psalm 63:1 – 4

Psalm 9:10

What you call God often reveals how well you know him.

If you seek God with all of your heart he will reveal himself to you (Deuteronomy 4:29; Ephesians 1:17 – 19).

Group Discussion **When You Believe in God but Don't Really Know Him** (5 Minutes)

Take a few minutes to talk about what you just watched.

1. What part of the teaching had the most impact on you?

2. How do you respond to the idea of "Christian Atheism"?

Individual Activity **How Well Do I Know God?** (5 Minutes)

Complete this activity on your own.

1. Briefly review the following list of statements and place a checkmark next to those you feel are true for you.

   ☐ I believe God loves everyone, but I sometimes struggle to believe that God loves me.

   ☐ I often feel disconnected from God.

   ☐ I pray when I need help, but I don't routinely spend time with God.

   ☐ I feel trapped in a cycle of shame about my past.

   ☐ I don't feel much need or desire to read the Bible.

   ☐ I sincerely believe in God, but I can't say I prioritize my life around him.

cont.

☐ I don't feel the same devotion to God as I did when I first became a Christian.

☐ There are some things about me that I know aren't what they should be, but I don't know if I can ever really change.

☐ My belief in God doesn't seem to keep me from worrying a lot.

☐ My lifestyle, actions, and decisions don't always line up with what I say I believe about God.

☐ I don't talk about my faith with people who don't believe in God.

☐ I don't experience worship or express praise to God in my daily life.

☐ I find it difficult to forgive people who have hurt me.

☐ My sense of security is impacted more by how I am doing financially than by how I am doing spiritually.

☐ I believe in God, but I'm not so big on the church.

☐ I'm not sure my heart breaks for the things that break the heart of God.

☐ I tend to diminish or overlook my sins and failures rather than grieving them.

☐ I don't often experience a passionate desire to please God.

☐ It feels like a long time since I've heard God's voice or experienced God's leading in my life.

☐ I sometimes feel God is not fair.

☐ It's rare for me to feel completely surrendered to God. Sometimes I'm not even sure I want to be.

2. Circle the two or three statements on the checklist that best describe where you're at spiritually right now. Or you may wish to write your own statement below.

3. Based on your responses from the checklist, circle the number on the continuum that best describes the degree to which you feel you know God.

1	2	3	4	5	6	7	8	9	10

I believe in God, but I don't know him.	I believe in God, but I don't know him well.	I believe in God, know him intimately, and serve him wholeheartedly.

Group Discussion (30 Minutes)

How Well Do I Know God?

1. Describe your experience of working through the checklist. For example, was it uncomfortable, confirming, surprising? Why?

2. How do you feel about the number you circled for question 3 in the Individual Activity? Would you say that the level at which you know God now is the highest it's ever been? Lowest? Somewhere in between?

3. If you feel comfortable, share one or more of the statements you circled on the checklist. Why do you think this statement is true for you right now?

Connecting Love and Obedience

Throughout the Old and New Testaments, the Bible makes a strong connection between knowing God and living for God. In an authentic relationship with God, it is impossible to separate love from obedience, belief from behavior, faith from practice. Each reinforces and balances the other.

4. Go around the group and have a different person read aloud each of the passages listed below. As the passages are read, underline any words or phrases that stand out to you. You may wish to read each passage twice to give everyone time to listen and respond.

> Know therefore that the Lord your God is God; he is the faithful God, keeping his covenant of love to a thousand generations of those who love him and keep his commandments (Deuteronomy 7:9).

> But be very careful to keep the commandment and the law that Moses the servant of the Lord gave you: to love the Lord your God, to walk in obedience to him, to keep his commands, to hold fast to him and to serve him with all your heart and with all your soul (Joshua 22:5).

cont.

If we are to be new people in Christ, then we must show our newness to the world. If we are to follow Christ, it must be in the way we spend each day.

WILLIAM LAW
A Serious Call to a Devout and Holy Life

Fine feelings, new insights, greater interest in "religion" mean nothing unless they make our actual behavior better; just as in an illness "feeling better" is not much good if the thermometer shows that your temperature is still going up.

C. S. LEWIS
Mere Christianity

The word obedient *comes from the Latin word* audire, *which means "listening." ... Jesus' life was a life of obedience.... Jesus was "all ear."*

HENRI J. M. NOUWEN
Making All Things New

Such people claim they know God, but they deny him by the way they live (Titus 1:16 NLT).

And we can be sure that we know him if we obey his commandments. If someone claims, "I know God," but doesn't obey God's commandments, that person is a liar and is not living in the truth. But those who obey God's word truly show how completely they love him. That is how we know we are living in him. Those who say they live in God should live their lives as Jesus did (1 John 2:3 – 6 NLT).

5. Based on these passages, how would you describe the connection between loving God and obeying God?

6. Describe the characteristics of someone trying to live one way or the other — loving God without obeying God or obeying God without loving God. In either case, what good things do you think the person might miss out on in their relationship with God?

7. Would you say you have experienced what the passages describe — obeying God out of love and loving God with your obedience? If so, describe your experience and how it's impacted you. If not, what would you say is the hardest part for you — obeying God out of love or loving God with your obedience?

Loving Obedience

8. If we affirm that failures to obey God are sin, the next challenge is how to overcome those failures in our lives. In *Surrender to Love*, author David Benner describes the role of God's love in helping us move from disobedience to obedience:

> My attachment to sinful ways of being is much too strong to ever be undone by mere willpower.... Genuine transformation requires vulnerability. It is not the fact of being loved unconditionally that is life-changing. It is the risky experience of *allowing myself* to be loved unconditionally.

If genuine transformation requires vulnerability, do you think disobedience could be described as a refusal to be vulnerable with God? Why or why not?

There is only one way to love God: to take not a single step without him, and to follow with a brave heart wherever he leads.

FRANÇOIS FÉNELON
Christian Perfection

What [God] desires is reverential intimacy. He wants us close enough to him that we know his heart — close enough to hear his heartbeat. He wants to look into our eyes, and he wants us to look into his.

DAVID G. BENNER
Surrender to Love

9. Would you say that you have had a risky experience of allowing yourself to be loved unconditionally by God? If you have and if you feel comfortable doing so, share that experience and the impact it has, or once had, on your ability to obey God. If not, what do you think prevents you from allowing yourself to be loved unconditionally by God?

Individual Activity What I Want to Remember (2 Minutes)

Complete this activity on your own.

1. Briefly review the outline and any notes you took.

2. In the space below, write down the most significant thing you gained in this session — from the teaching, activities, or discussions.

   What I want to remember from this session ...

Closing Prayer

Close your time together with prayer.

✝ Between-Sessions Personal Study

● READ AND REFLECT

Read the introduction and chapter 1 of *The Christian Atheist*. Use the space below to note any insights or questions you want to bring to the next group session.

● MAKING IT PERSONAL

A Christian Atheist might sound like someone who's got a faith problem or perhaps at least a spiritual confusion issue. But the core problem for the Christian Atheist isn't belief; it's intimacy. The Christian Atheist doesn't really know God very well.

> Belief isn't the same as personal knowledge.
> *The Christian Atheist*, page 33

1. Think about your closest relationship. Of the following list of factors, which *three* would you say have been most important in keeping it strong and growing?

☐ Time together   ☐ Acceptance
☐ Having fun   ☐ Talking things through
☐ Respect   ☐ Forgiveness
☐ Honesty   ☐ Trust
☐ Vulnerability   ☐ Loyalty
☐ Communication   ☐ Fighting fair
☐ Shared interests   ☐ Support/encouragement
☐ Generosity   ☐ Kindness
☐ Compassion   ☐ Other:

Write the three items you identified on the checklist in the left column on the chart below. Use the remaining columns to describe why this factor has been important in your closest relationship and how you experience it in your relationship with God.

RELATIONSHIP FACTOR	WHY THIS HAS BEEN IMPORTANT IN MY CLOSEST RELATIONSHIP	HOW I EXPERIENCE THIS IN MY RELATIONSHIP WITH GOD
Example *Time together*	**Example** *We've shared a lot of different experiences and we've seen each other at our best and our worst. It's built a lot of history and trust between us.*	**Example** *I'm not as intentional about spending time with God. I do try to check in with him throughout the day, but I sometimes forget.*

What stands out most to you when you consider the similarities and differences in your closest personal relationship and your relationship with God?

What two or three things have you learned in your closest personal relationship that might help you to seek God and get to know him better?

•

•

•

God cares about how we live. And a relationship with God naturally will flow out in daily attitudes and actions. So if you *look* good, you *are* good, right? Well, maybe not. Knowing God can lead to a positive lifestyle, but the reverse isn't true. Our outward actions alone don't prove that we enjoy an inward relationship with God. Just because we *do* good doesn't mean we know the One who *is* good.

The Christian Atheist, page 35 – 36

2. Knowing God requires more of us than simply believing God exists (James 2:19). And it requires more of us than dutiful adherence to Christian rules (Galatians 4:6 – 11). Knowing God requires loving obedience, an obedience that comes from the heart.

> Anyone who loves me will obey my teaching. My Father will love them, and we will come to them and make our home with them. Anyone who does not love me will not obey my teaching. These words you hear are not my own; they belong to the Father who sent me (John 14:23 – 24).

> But thanks be to God that, though you used to be slaves to sin, you have come to *obey from your heart* the pattern of teaching that has now claimed your allegiance (Romans 6:17, emphasis added).

John used the image of a home to describe the intimacy of the relationship God wants with us. Place an X on the continuum below to indicate the degree to which obeying Christ's teaching has allowed God to make his home with you.

Disobedience consistently crowds God out of my heart.	Obedience consistently allows God to be at home in my heart.

In Romans, the apostle Paul spoke of obeying God from the heart. Place an X on the continuum below to indicate the degree to which you feel this is true for you.

I do not obey from the heart. My obedience is inconsistent and/or motivated primarily by things like habit, heart, or duty.	**I obey from the heart.** My obedience is motivated primarily by my love for God.

Based on your responses on the two continuums, would you say your experiences of obedience (or disobedience) are drawing your heart closer to God or pulling your heart farther away from God?

How do you imagine your life might change if love for God more consistently motivated your actions and decisions? Overall, would you say these are changes you'd be eager or reluctant to experience? Why?

> As you get to know him better, you will change.
> *The Christian Atheist*, page 43

3. God is in the transformation business. The more we get to know him, the more his love changes us. He brings healing and wholeness that enables us to rest in his love and to follow him *whole*heartedly. Here is how the prophet Ezekiel described God's heart-changing promise:

> And I will give them singleness of heart and put a new spirit within them. I will take away their stony, stubborn heart and give them a tender, responsive heart, so they will obey my decrees and regulations. Then they will truly be my people, and I will be their God (Ezekiel 11:19 – 20 NLT).

In what ways, if any, would you say your heart might be divided, stony or stubborn toward God?

Write a brief prayer asking God to honor his Ezekiel promise by giving you an undivided heart — a heart that is tender and responsive to him.

Getting to know God isn't difficult, and it isn't about a bunch of rules. Yes, God wants your obedience, but he wants your heart even more. He loves you so much. Surrender yourself to that love, and it will be certain death for Christian Atheism — a death that will lead to a whole new life of knowing God.

When You Believe in God but Don't Think He's Fair

FAIR
[fair]
free from bias, dishonesty, or injustice

DESERVING
[dih-**zur**-ving]
worthy to receive something because of need, merit, or justice

SUFFERING
[suhf-er-ing]
physical or psychological pain and distress

COMFORT
[**kuhm**-fert]
to provide consolation; relief from distress or anxiety

GOOD
[good]
having an upright and virtuous character; worthy of honor or high esteem

JUST
[juhst]
righteous; guided by truth, reason, and justice

Group Discussion Checking In (5 Minutes)

Welcome to session 2 of *The Christian Atheist*. A key part of getting to know God better is sharing your journey with others. Before watching the video, briefly check in with each other about your experiences since the last session. For example:

- What insights did you discover in the personal study or in the chapters you read from *The Christian Atheist* book?
- How did the last session impact your daily life or your relationship with God?
- What questions would you like to ask the other members of your group?

Video When You Believe in God but Don't Think He's Fair (18 Minutes)

Play the video segment for session 2. As you watch, use the outline below to follow along or to take notes on anything that stands out to you.

Notes

Have you ever asked God, "Why do you let so many bad things happen?"

Three things to remember when you don't understand something about God:

1. We don't deserve good things.

If you think you're good, Jesus didn't come for you (Mark 2:17).

We are not good in the eyes of God (Romans 3:10 – 12; 6:23).

2. Good things happen to bad people.

God does not treat us as our sins deserve (Psalm 103:10 – 12).

3. God is present in your pain.

The Lord is a God of comfort (Isaiah 49:13).

God isn't fair. He doesn't give us what our sins deserve. He is higher. He is working in all things to bring about good.

Group Discussion | **When You Believe in God but Don't Think He's Fair** (5 Minutes)

Take a few minutes to talk about what you just watched.

1. What part of the teaching had the most impact on you?

2. Has the question of God's fairness been a significant issue for you? Why or why not?

Individual Activity   Three Things to Remember (3 Minutes)

Complete this activity on your own.

1. On the video, Craig presents three things to remember when we don't understand something about God: (1) we don't deserve good things, (2) good things happen to bad people, and (3) God is present in your pain. For each of the following statements, circle the number that indicates the degree to which you agree or disagree.

   We don't deserve good things. Because of our sinfulness, we deserve punishment (Romans 6:23).

I disagree completely.	I disagree somewhat.	I'm not sure whether I agree or disagree.	I agree somewhat.	I agree completely.

   Good things happen to bad people. It's a good thing God is not fair because then he would give us what we deserve (Psalm 103:10 – 12). Instead, he gives us grace.

I disagree completely.	I disagree somewhat.	I'm not sure whether I agree or disagree.	I agree somewhat.	I agree completely.

   God is present in your pain. When you hurt, your heavenly Father hurts with you and longs to comfort you (Isaiah 49:13).

I disagree completely.	I disagree somewhat.	I'm not sure whether I agree or disagree.	I agree somewhat.	I agree completely.

2. Based on your answers to the three statements in question 1, respond to the appropriate statement below.

   If you mostly *agreed*, to what degree do you still struggle with the issue of God's fairness?

This is not a struggle for me.	This is rarely a struggle for me.	I'm not sure if this is a struggle for me or not.	This is sometimes a struggle for me.	This is a significant struggle for me.

If you mostly *disagreed*, to what degree do you still struggle with the issue of God's fairness?

1	2	3	4	5
This is not a struggle for me.	This is rarely a struggle for me.	I'm not sure if this is a struggle for me or not.	This is sometimes a struggle for me.	This is a significant struggle for me.

Group Discussion (27 Minutes)

Three Things to Remember

1. Do you tend to agree or disagree with the three statements from question 1 of the Individual Activity?

2. How does your overall agreement or disagreement impact your perspective on whether or not you think God is fair?

We Don't Deserve Good Things

3. Here is the common logic that leads people to think God is unfair: *Bad things should happen to bad people and good things should happen to good people. I am a good person so I deserve good things.* Scripture counters this logic. In fact, the Bible states it is our inherent lack of goodness that made it necessary for Jesus to die for our sins:

> There is no one righteous, not even one; there is no one who understands; there is no one who seeks God. All have turned away, they have together become worthless; there is no one who does good, not even one (Romans 3:10–12).

> "Why do you call me good?" Jesus answered. "No one is good — except God alone" (Luke 18:19).

> Jesus said to them, "It is not the healthy who need a doctor, but the sick. I have not come to call the righteous, but sinners" (Mark 2:17).

cont.

> *Those who would like the God of scripture to be more purely ethical, do not know what they ask.*
>
> C.S. LEWIS
> *The Problem of Pain*

> *If I care to listen, I get a loud whisper from the gospel that I did not get what I deserved. I deserved punishment and got forgiveness. I deserved wrath and got love. I deserved debtor's prison and got instead a clean credit history. I deserved stern lectures and crawl-on-your-knees repentance; I got a banquet — Babette's feast — spread for me.*
>
> PHILIP YANCEY
> *What's So Amazing about Grace?*

If you have accepted Christ, what was it that convinced you of your lack of goodness and your need for forgiveness? If you have not accepted Christ, is it difficult to think of yourself as someone who is not good and needs forgiveness? Why or why not?

Good Things Happen to Bad People

4. Once we acknowledge our failures and our need for God, we actually get some amazing news:

> He does not treat us as our sins deserve or repay us according to our iniquities. For as high as the heavens are above the earth, so great is his love for those who fear him; as far as the east is from the west, so far has he removed our transgressions from us (Psalm 103:10 – 12).

> I — yes, I alone — will blot out your sins for my own sake and will never think of them again (Isaiah 43:25 NLT).

On the video, Craig said he was so happy when the judge blotted out his speeding ticket that he practically danced all the way to his car. How does your awareness of God's goodness and mercy inspire joy or gratitude in you?

God Is Present in Your Pain

5. When you experience disappointment, loss, or tragedy, do you tend to run toward God for help and comfort or to pull away from God in hurt and anger? If you feel comfortable, briefly share an experience that shows how you respond to God when life is hard.

> *Those who are totally converted come to every experience and ask not whether or not they liked it, but what does it have to teach them. "What's the message in this for me? What's the gift in this for me? How is God in this event? Where is God in this suffering?"*
>
> RICHARD ROHR
> *Everything Belongs*

> *"The LORD will keep you from all evil" [Psalm 121:7]. The promise of the psalm ... is not that we shall never stub our toes, but that no injury, no illness, no accident, no distress will have evil power over us, that is, will be able to separate us from God's purposes in us.*
>
> EUGENE H. PETERSON
> *A Long Obedience in the Same Direction*

6. Scripture affirms that God's goodness is unchanging, that he is present with us when we are hurting, and that he is always working to redeem our suffering:

> The LORD is good, a refuge in times of trouble. He cares for those who trust in him (Nahum 1:7).

> But those who suffer he delivers in their suffering; he speaks to them in their affliction (Job 36:15).

> [God] works out everything in conformity with the purpose of his will (Ephesians 1:11).

Which of these truths is most meaningful or comforting to you? Why?

How might your perspective change if the questions you routinely asked in hardships were, "How is God in this suffering?" or "What's the gift in this for me?" rather than "Why is God so unfair to me?"

Individual Activity What I Want to Remember (2 Minutes)

Complete this activity on your own.

1. Briefly review the outline and any notes you took.

2. In the space below, write down the most significant thing you gained in this session — from the teaching, activities, or discussions.

   What I want to remember from this session . . .

Closing Prayer

Close your time together with prayer.

✝ Between-Sessions Personal Study

● READ AND REFLECT

Read chapters 4, 5, and 6 of *The Christian Atheist*. Use the space below to note any insights or questions you want to bring to the next group session.

● GOD IS GOOD — ALL THE TIME

Fairness is an excellent principle when we're good, but an unfortunate principle when we're not so good. And when it comes to God, we are pretty much always going to be on the not-so-good side of the fairness equation. But we can be glad that God is not fair; we don't get what we deserve. Instead of punishment we get death-defying grace. And we get God with us, especially in the midst of life's most difficult and painful experiences.

> I'm usually quick to ask why something bad happens. Rarely do I stop to ask why God might bless me with something good. The truth is, good things happen to people like you and me, people who are sinful and deserve death.
>
> *The Christian Atheist*, page 105

1. During an average week, how would you describe the level of your gratitude for the good things God has done for you?

  ☐ I rarely express my gratitude to God.
  ☐ I occasionally express my gratitude to God.
  ☐ I sometimes express my gratitude to God.
  ☐ I frequently express my gratitude to God.
  ☐ I continuously express my gratitude to God.

More specifically, how would you describe the level of your gratitude for God's goodness in forgiving your sins? Do you find it easy to be routinely grateful for God's forgiveness or do you sometimes take it for granted?

2. On the video, Craig says, "[We can] thank God he is not fair. If he were fair, he would give us what we deserve [death]. Instead, he gives us grace, which is something we don't deserve" (Psalm 103:10 – 12). How does this perspective impact your view of God's fairness?

Humanly, we may never understand. All we know is that God is always good.... We can take comfort in knowing that God's ways are higher than our ways.... He is working in all things to bring about good.

The Christian Atheist video

The Bible is full of stories of suffering and how God miraculously snatches good from the jaws of evil. Perhaps one of the most powerful is the story of Joseph (Genesis 37, 39 – 50). After being betrayed by his brothers and sold into slavery in Egypt, Joseph was just beginning to prosper when he was falsely accused of sexual assault and imprisoned. People who promised to help him forgot their promises and he remained behind bars — for years. Eventually he came to the attention of the Pharaoh, who was so impressed with Joseph's honesty and wisdom that he put this former slave in charge of his entire country.

3. God didn't prevent the years of betrayal and pain Joseph experienced, but he was actively at work in Joseph's suffering. Read Genesis 39:2 – 3, 21, 23. Based on these verses, how would you describe the work God did in the midst of Joseph's hardships?

In what ways, if any, do you recognize that the Lord is with you now, at work in your life in the midst of whatever difficulties you face? If it's hard for you to recognize how God is with you, in what ways do you wish you could experience God with you now?

4. After Joseph was reconciled with the brothers who long ago betrayed him, they asked his forgiveness and offered themselves to be his slaves. Joseph was deeply moved and reassured his brothers:

> Don't be afraid. Am I in the place of God? You intended to harm me, but God intended it for good to accomplish what is now being done, the saving of many lives (Genesis 50:19 – 20).

Joseph didn't deny the reality of the harm he experienced, but he affirmed how God transformed intentional evil into exponential good. Have you had an experience in which God transformed something painful or bad in your life into something good? If so, how does that experience impact your ability to trust that God is at work in the things you struggle with now? If not, how do you feel about the idea of looking for signs of God's activity and goodness in the painful experience you struggle with most?

5. Although there are some things we may never understand this side of heaven, the Bible teaches that, like Joseph, we do experience God's goodness here on earth:

> I remain confident of this: I will see the goodness of the LORD in the land of the living. Wait for the LORD; be strong and take heart and wait for the LORD (Psalm 27:13 – 14).

> The LORD is good to those whose hope is in him, to the one who seeks him; it is good to wait quietly for the salvation of the LORD (Lamentations 3:25 – 26).

According to these verses, there are times when seeing God's goodness requires waiting. The sense of the word used for "wait" in Hebrew is not a passive waiting but a hopeful, expectant waiting. In your current struggles, how would you describe the difference between waiting passively and waiting expectantly to see God's goodness? How do you hope to experience God's goodness?

God is not fair, but he is good. And unlike fairness, there is no wrong side to the goodness equation when it comes to God. When you don't deserve it, God is good. When you've messed up and need forgiveness, God is good. When you're afraid and lonely, God is good. When you're hurting and life makes no sense, God is still good. God is good — all the time. All the time … (wait for it) … God is good!

When You Believe in God but Aren't Sure He Loves You

GUILT
[gilt]
having committed an offense, crime, violation, or wrong

SHAME
[sheym]
a painful feeling arising from the consciousness of something dishonorable, improper, ridiculous

INSIGNIFICANCE
[in-sig-**nif**-i-k*uh*ns]
lack of importance, consequence, status

LOVE
[luhv]
a profoundly tender, passionate affection

UNCONDITIONAL
[uhn-k*uh*n-**dish**-*uh*-nl]
without limits or conditions; absolute; total

EVERLASTING
[ev-er-**las**-ting, -**lah**-sting]
never failing or coming to an end

BELOVED
[bih-**luhv**-id, -**luhvd**]
somebody who is loved very much

Group Discussion   Checking In (5 Minutes)

Welcome to session 3 of *The Christian Atheist*. A key part of getting to know God better is sharing your journey with each other. Before watching the video, briefly check in with each other about your experiences since the last session. For example:

- What insights did you discover in the personal study or in the chapters you read from *The Christian Atheist* book?
- How did the last session impact your daily life or your relationship with God?
- What questions would you like to ask the other members of your group?

Video   When You Believe in God but Aren't Sure He Loves You
(17 Minutes)

Play the video segment for session 3. As you watch, use the outline below to follow along or to take notes on anything that stands out to you.

Notes

Two questions Christian Atheists ask:

1. "Why would God love someone as bad as me?" (Job 42:5 – 6).

2. "How could God love someone so insignificant?" (Exodus 3:11).

Love isn't just what God *does*; love is who God *is* (1 John 4:8 – 10).

Two benefits of the love of God:

1. God's love covers our sins (1 Peter 4:8; Titus 3:4 – 5).

2. God's love makes us significant. (Jeremiah 31:3; Luke 15; John 3:16).

God will tell you he loves you if you pause and listen.

When you receive that love and stop trying to earn it, it totally changes the way you live.

We love because he first loved us (1 John 4:19).

Group Discussion **When You Believe in God but Aren't Sure He Loves You** (5 Minutes)

Take a few minutes to talk about what you just watched.

1. What part of the teaching had the most impact on you?

2. Which struggle do you relate to more — believing that God could love someone as bad as you, or believing God could love someone as insignificant as you?

Partner Activity Characteristics of God's Love (12 Minutes)

1. Pair up with one other person.

2. Take turns reading aloud each of the following passages. After each passage, come up with one word or a brief phrase that summarizes the characteristic(s) of God and God's love the passage describes. For example: *sacrificial, merciful, beyond comprehension, eternal.*

   Romans 5:8

   Isaiah 38:17

   Psalm 103:8 – 12

   Psalm 89:1 – 2

   1 John 4:15 – 16

   Romans 8:35 – 39

Group Discussion (19 Minutes)

God's Love Covers Our Sins

1. Of the characteristics of God you listed in the Partner Activity, which is most meaningful to you? Why?

2. The prophet Isaiah wrote, "You have put all my sins behind your back" (Isaiah 38:17). If God removes our sins from his sight — literally putting them behind him — why do you think we sometimes run around God to snatch them back? In other words, why might we resist putting our sins behind us even when God has forgiven us?

3. What most often undermines your ability to believe in God's love and forgiveness?

4. What most reassures you and helps you to believe deep down that you are loved and forgiven by God (for example: biblical truths, a personal experience, regular time spent alone with God, etc.)?

God's Love Makes Us Significant

5. What do you think it means, in practical terms, to "know and rely on the love God has for us" (1 John 4:16)?

6. In what ways, if any, would you say that God has communicated his love and care for you specifically? It may have been recently or long ago, something simple or something more significant, but you experienced it as an "I love you," from God.

> *Our hunger for significance is a signal of who we are and why we are here, and it also is the basis of humanity's enduring response to Jesus. For he always takes individual human beings as seriously as their shredded dignity demands, and he has the resources to carry through with his high estimate of them.*
>
> DALLAS WILLARD
> *The Divine Conspiracy*

7. In Romans 8:35 – 39, the apostle Paul offered a list of things that cannot separate us from the love of Christ: *trouble, hardship, persecution, famine, nakedness, danger, sword, death, life, angels, demons, the present, the future, any powers, neither height nor depth, nor anything else in all creation.* Which item best represents an area in your life in which you are struggling to experience God's love? For example, perhaps an uncertain future has you feeling vulnerable and alone. If you feel comfortable doing so, briefly describe the situation and how you think it might be different if you could experience God's love in it.

Individual Activity What I Want to Remember (2 Minutes)

Complete this activity on your own.

1. Briefly review the outline and any notes you took.

2. In the space below, write down the most significant thing you gained in this session — from the teaching, activities, or discussions.

What I want to remember from this session ...

Closing Prayer

Close your time together with prayer.

Between-Sessions Personal Study

● READ AND REFLECT

Read chapters 2 and 3 of *The Christian Atheist*. Use the space below to note any insights or questions you want to bring to the next group session.

● GENUINE HEART CONVICTION

One of the first Bible verses many Christians memorize is all about love: "For God so loved the world that he gave his one and only Son, so that whoever believes in him shall not perish but have eternal life" (John 3:16). It's a foundational truth every new believer claims, but one that Christian Atheists sometimes struggle to fully embrace. The journey out of Christian Atheism begins when we move from saying, "I believe God so loved the world," to saying, "I believe God so loved me ... I am God's beloved."

> This is the root of a challenge for many Christian Atheists: belief in God doesn't automatically result in the belief — the genuine heart conviction — that God loves us.... We Christian Atheists can easily believe that God loves other people; we just can't comprehend how or why he'd love *us*.
>
> *The Christian Atheist*, page 60

1. How strong is your heart conviction that God really loves you? Circle the number that best describes your response.

| 2 | 3 | 4 | 5 | 6 | 7 | 8 | 9 | 10 |

UNLOVED	SORTA LOVED	BELOVED
I don't believe God loves me	I believe God loves other people, but I struggle to believe God loves me.	I believe God loves me.

Based on the number you chose, respond to one of the two sets of questions below.

If you chose 1 – 6: What is it that makes it difficult for you to believe that God loves you? What do you imagine the most significant change in your life might be if you could believe God loves you?

If you chose 7 – 10: What key truth, insight, or experience has helped you to really believe God loves you? How would you say God has demonstrated his love for you personally?

2. Believing in God's love with heart conviction isn't something we can force ourselves to do. But we can spend time with God and steep ourselves in truths about how much he loves us. This is one way we "let the message of Christ dwell among [us] richly" (Colossians 3:16). Following are four passages about God's love. Briefly review these passages in your Bible and choose one to focus on.

| Psalm 25:6 – 7 | Psalm 59:16 – 17 |
| Psalm 51:1 – 2 | Romans 8:35 – 39 |

Following the prompts below, read through your chosen passage a total of four times. Each time, read the passage slowly and aloud. Allow one to two minutes of quiet listening after each reading as you reflect on the question for that reading. Quiet listening is an essential part of the process — don't skip it! Allow yourself to enjoy spending unhurried time alone with God. Then use the space provided to note your response.

As you begin, allow yourself a few moments of silence to quiet your heart and enter into God's presence. Thank God for being with you and invite him to speak to you through the passage.

• Read the passage for the first time. What word or phrase captures your attention?

- Read the passage again. Consider how this passage relates to your life right now. What do you think God may be asking you to do?

- Read the passage once more. What do you want to say to God?

- Read the passage for the final time. Rest in God's love for you.
- Close your time with a brief prayer, thanking God for his love and for his goodness to you.

> Why would God love you? Because that's who God is: he's love. And that makes you who you are: beloved.
>
> *The Christian Atheist*, page 71

3. God's love for you is powerful — it covers your sins. God's love for you is personal — it graces you with significance. God says, "I've never quit loving you and never will. Expect love, love, and more love!" (Jeremiah 31:3 MSG). How do you respond to this promise of unfailing love? What comfort, hope, encouragement, or reassurance does it inspire in you?

Surrendering to God's love changes everything. As author and pastor John Ortberg writes, "We cannot be loved without being changed." It's a package deal. Give God the dark and tangled mess of your life and he gives you life-changing love. Offer up your hurt and confusion and he gives you love. Hand over your guilt and insignificance and he gives you more love. That's transformation. That's what it means to be God's beloved.

When You Believe in God but Trust More in Money

TRUST
[truhst]
reliance on the integrity, strength, ability, surety, etc., of a person or thing

MONEY
[**muhn**-ee]
any medium of exchange used as a measure of value

WORSHIP
[**wur**-ship]
to treat somebody or something as divine and show respect by engaging in acts of adoration and devotion

SERVE
[surv]
to work for someone; to render obedience or homage to

CONTENTMENT
[k*uh*n-**tent**-m*uh*nt]
not wanting more or anything else; calm satisfaction; ease of mind

GENEROUS
[**jen**-er-*uh*s]
willing to give money, help, or time freely; kind, openhanded, unselfish

Group Discussion Checking In (5 Minutes)

Welcome to session 4 of *The Christian Atheist*. A key part of getting to know God better is sharing your journey with each other. Before watching the video, briefly check in with each other about your experiences since the last session. For example:

- What insights did you discover in the personal study or in the chapters you read from *The Christian Atheist* book?
- How did the last session impact your daily life or your relationship with God?
- What questions would you like to ask the other members of your group?

Video When You Believe in God but Trust More in Money (18 Minutes)

Play the video segment for session 4. As you watch, use the outline below to follow along or to take notes on anything that stands out to you.

Notes

The number-one competitor for our hearts is money (Luke 16:13).

Two ways we trust in money:

1. We trust money to provide happiness.

2. We trust money to provide security.

Two rich men who encountered Christ:

1. A rich young ruler (Matthew 19:21 – 22)

2. A tax collector named Zacchaeus (Luke 19:8)

The challenge is: we are one of these two men.

When you fall in love with Jesus, two things will happen every time:

1. You become strangely content (1 Timothy 6:17).

2. You become irrationally generous.

The problem with Christian Atheists is they love and serve money and use God.

When you truly get to know God, you will love and worship and serve him.

Group Discussion — When You Believe in God but Trust More in Money (5 Minutes)

Take a few minutes to talk about what you just watched.

1. What part of the teaching had the most impact on you?

2. How do you respond to the idea that money is the number-one competitor for our hearts?

Individual Activity — Money and Me (4 Minutes)

Complete this activity on your own.

For each of the following statements, check the box that best describes your response.

1. My spending style might best be described as ...

   ☐ Tightfisted, stingy, grudging
   ☐ Cautious, thrifty, frugal
   ☐ Moderate, planned, sensible
   ☐ Spontaneous, risky, carefree
   ☐ Extravagant, extreme, unrestrained

2. My giving style might best be described as ...

   ☐ Tightfisted, stingy, grudging
   ☐ Cautious, thrifty, frugal
   ☐ Moderate, planned, sensible
   ☐ Spontaneous, risky, carefree
   ☐ Extravagant, extreme, unrestrained

3. If the details of my finances were made public, I would feel:

   ☐ Mortified
   ☐ Embarrassed
   ☐ Ambivalent
   ☐ Unconcerned
   ☐ Honored

4. My use of money — earning, saving, giving, spending, use of credit/debt — demonstrates my belief that God owns everything and I am a steward or trustee of his resources. This statement is:

☐ Almost never true of me
☐ Rarely true of me
☐ Occasionally true of me
☐ Often true of me
☐ Almost always true of me

5. If I had to live the rest of my life with just enough money for basic necessities — adequate food, shelter, clothing — it would:

☐ Pretty much eliminate my ability to be happy.
☐ Significantly limit my ability to be happy.
☐ Occasionally limit my ability to be happy.
☐ Have a small impact on my ability to be happy.
☐ Have almost no impact on my ability to be happy.

Group Discussion (26 Minutes)

Money and Me

1. Overall, how would you describe your comfort level when it comes to talking about money in connection with your faith?

2. Describe your experience of responding to the questions in the Individual Activity. For example, was it uncomfortable, sobering, educational, reassuring? Why?

I grew up in the Bible Belt. When I became a Christian, I learned I didn't have to stop buying stuff I just had to start buying Christian stuff.

SHANE CLAIBORNE
@claibornequotes on Twitter

[A wallet] looks like a piece of leather but it's really the temple of the twenty-first century.... We give this little piece of leather the power to make us feel secure, successful, and valuable. It is very hard for us to surrender control of this little piece of leather. The real issue: who's in charge? Are you holding it or is it holding you?

JOHN ORTBERG
When the Game Is Over, It All Goes Back in the Box

3. What differences, if any, did you discover between your spending style and your giving style?

Two Rich Guys

4. Read aloud Matthew 19:16 – 22 and Luke 19:1 – 10. Discuss the similarities and differences between the rich young ruler and Zacchaeus.

   • What would you say both men had in common?

   • What was the apparent spiritual condition of each man before meeting Jesus?

   • How did money/possessions mark a spiritual turning point for each man?

5. A "functional savior" is anything or anyone we choose over Christ. For the rich young ruler, it was possessions. On the video, Craig gave other examples of how we put Christ second: choosing television over prayer, spending more on coffee than giving to the church, thinking about how to *get* more money rather than how to *give* more money. In what ways do you sometimes choose other things over Christ?

Contentment and Generosity

6. On the video, Craig says, "When you truly fall in love with Jesus, you become strangely content; what money buys doesn't have as much power over you." How do you understand the connection between the level of intimacy in your relationship with Christ and the level of contentment you experience? If you feel comfortable doing so, share an experience that illustrates your response.

> *Faith means you want God and want to want nothing else.*
>
> BRENNAN MANNING
> *The Ragamuffin Gospel*
>
> *Unless you have already put God first ... what you will have to do to be financially secure, impress other people, or fulfill your desires will invariably lead you against God's wishes.*
>
> DALLAS WILLARD
> *The Divine Conspiracy*

7. Read 1 Timothy 6:17 – 19 aloud. Do you know someone whose life demonstrates what it means to "do good, to be rich in good deeds, and to be generous and willing to share" (v. 18)? What characteristics do you admire most about this person?

8. When it comes to tithing, it's been said that 10 percent is a good place to start but a tragic place to stop. What concerns you and what excites you about the idea of rearranging your life so that you could give more?

Individual Activity **What I Want to Remember** (2 Minutes)

Complete this activity on your own.

1. Briefly review the outline and any notes you took.

2. In the space below, write down the most significant thing you gained in this session — from the teaching, activities, or discussions.

   What I want to remember from this session …

Closing Prayer

Close your time together with prayer.

✝ Between-Sessions Personal Study

● READ AND REFLECT

Read chapters 10, 11, and 12 of *The Christian Atheist*. Use the space below to note any insights or questions you want to bring to the next group session.

● LOVING ATTACHMENTS

We Christian Atheists can develop an attachment disorder. Something goes wrong with our spiritual Velcro and the attachment we're meant to have with God gets snagged on lesser things. Money is among the hardest attachments to break, especially when it's tied up with our hopes for security and happiness. But God invites us to let it go, to surrender our confidence in money and to attach ourselves in loving trust to him alone.

> For the Christian Atheist money can become a functional savior.... [It is] the number-one competitor for our hearts.... Many of us, if we are really honest, would say, "In this part of my life I am a Christian Atheist. I believe, at least by my actions, that money will buy me happiness or money will buy me security. I don't like it, but I have to admit I believe in God but, ultimately, I trust in money."
>
> *The Christian Atheist* video

1. Congratulations! You just received one million dollars. The taxes are paid and you are free and clear to use the money as you wish.

   What is the biggest financial issue the money would solve for you?

In what ways would the money enable you to have greater peace of mind?

How would you describe the impact one million dollars would have on your overall happiness and your sense of security?

2. How would you describe the impact your relationship with Christ has on your overall happiness and sense of security?

In what ways is the peace of mind you experience in your relationship with Christ similar to or different from the peace of mind you might experience in receiving one million dollars?

How would you describe the level of trust you have that God will help you with the biggest financial issue you identified in question 1?

3. What similarities or differences do you notice in how you view money and how you view your relationship with Christ (questions 1 and 2)?

When we learn to trust in God alone, he is the one who provides us with what matters and lasts. Suddenly the earthly possessions that once gripped us don't hold us like they used to. Instead of seeing what we have as belonging to us, we see it as available to God for his use and his glory.

The Christian Atheist, page 186

4. A foundational biblical principle about money is that everything we have belongs to God and we are managers or trustees of God's resources.

> "The silver is mine and the gold is mine," declares the LORD Almighty (Haggai 2:8).

> For every animal of the forest is mine, and the cattle on a thousand hills (Psalm 50:10).

> The earth is the LORD's, and everything in it, the world, and all who live in it (Psalm 24:1).

> A person who is put in charge as a manager must be faithful (1 Corinthians 4:2 NLT).

> If you are faithful in little things, you will be faithful in large ones. But if you are dishonest in little things, you won't be honest with greater responsibilities. And if you are untrustworthy about worldly wealth, who will trust you with the true riches of heaven? And if you are not faithful with other people's things, why should you be trusted with things of your own? (Luke 16:10 – 12 NLT).

Reflect on your use of money over the last five to seven days. Overall, how would you characterize your decisions as God's money manager (consider your giving, saving, and debt as well as spending)? Would you say you made excellent, adequate, or poor decisions?

What positive aspects of this biblical principle — that God owns everything and we are trustees — appeal to you? What potential benefits can you identify?

When you fall in love with Jesus, you become strangely content [and] ... irrationally generous.... The more you love, worship, and serve God, the less money will have a grip on you.

The Christian Atheist video

5. Circle three to five words (total) from the lists below that characterize the kind of contentment or lack of contentment you currently feel about your finances.

Contentment	Lack of Contentment
Satisfaction	Discomfort
Ease	Misery
Peace	Unhappiness
Fulfillment	Sadness
Gladness	Unrest
Serenity	Dissatisfaction
Enjoyment	Annoyance
Quiet	Distress
Rest	Unease
Comfort	Disturbance
Order	Worry
Security	Agitation

In what ways might the words you circled also characterize your relationship with God?

6. The Christian Atheist believes in God but trusts more in money. This verse from Hebrews provides a clue about one reason why this might happen:

> Keep your lives free from the love of money and be content with what you have, because God has said, "Never will I leave you; never will I forsake you" (Hebrews 13:5).

Based on this verse, what fear does God seem to be addressing with his promise? Is this a fear you experience?

7. Do you sense any invitation from God to trust and rely on him more with your money? If so, what do you think God might be asking you to do?

When we learn to trust in God alone, he is the one who provides us with what matters and lasts. Suddenly the earthly possessions that once gripped us don't hold us like they used to. We are free! No longer responsible for masterminding our own security or happiness, we discover contentment at last and rest secure in God's loving care and provision.

When You Believe in God but Pursue Happiness at Any Cost

MORE
[mawr, mohr]
in greater quantity, amount, measure, degree, or number

HAPPINESS
[**hap**-ee-nis]
pleasure; contentment; joy; delight; exhilaration; enjoyment

MATERIALISM
[m*uh*-**teer**-ee-*uh*-liz-*uh*m]
devotion to material wealth and possessions at the expense of spiritual or intellectual values

BLESSED
[**bles**-id; blest]
divinely or supremely favored; fortunate

SATISFIED
[**sat**-is-fahyd]
content

ENOUGH
[ih-**nuhf**]
as much as is needed; sufficient

Group Discussion Checking In (5 Minutes)

Welcome to session 5 of *The Christian Atheist*. A key part of getting to know God better is sharing your journey with each other. Before watching the video, briefly check in with each other about your experiences since the last session. For example:

- What insights did you discover in the personal study or in the chapters you read from *The Christian Atheist* book?
- How did the last session impact your daily life or your relationship with God?
- What questions would you like to ask the other members of your group?

Video When You Believe in God but Pursue Happiness at Any Cost (17 Minutes)

Play the video segment for session 5. As you watch, use the outline below to follow along or to take notes on anything that stands out to you.

Notes

Three different times God doesn't want you to be happy:

1. God doesn't want you happy when it causes you to do something wrong or unwise.

2. God doesn't want you happy when it's only based on the things of this world.

Our happiness formula: better possessions + peaceful circumstances + thrilling experiences + right relationships + perfect appearance = happiness

The Bible says, "Do not love the world or anything in the world" (1 John 2:15 – 17).

3. God doesn't want you happy, he wants you blessed.

Makarios [ma-KAR-ee-os] is a Greek word in the Bible that means "supremely blessed" and "more than happy."

"Blessed [more than happy] is the [one] who fears the LORD, who finds great delight in his commands" (Psalm 112:1).

When you lower your expectations of this world and instead pursue God, then you can be more than happy.

The more you fall in love with God, the less the things of this world will pull you and draw you.

Our happiness is based on the goodness of God.

Group Discussion — When You Believe in God but Pursue Happiness at Any Cost (5 Minutes)

Take a few minutes to talk about what you just watched.

1. What part of the teaching had the most impact on you?

2. How do you respond to the idea that there is not a new thing that is ever going to make you happy or ultimately satisfy you?

Individual Activity — What Makes Me Happy (5 Minutes)

Complete this activity on your own.

1. For each of the items listed below, use the space provided to rate the degree to which you associate increased happiness with that item. Use the following scale:

> 3 = I almost always think this will make me happier.
> 2 = I frequently think this will make me happier.
> 1 = I occasionally think this will make me happier.
> 0 = I rarely think this will make me happier.

_____ Better possessions

_____ Peaceful circumstances

_____ Thrilling experiences

_____ The right relationships

_____ The perfect appearance

2. Circle one of the items you rated as a 2 or 3 in question 1 and insert it in the first blank below. Then complete the sentences.

If I could have _____ tomorrow, the biggest change in my life would be _____
_____.

This would make me happier because _____
_____.

Group Discussion (26 Minutes)

What Makes Me Happy

1. Based on the Individual Activity, what did you identify that would make you happier? Why do you think it would it make you happier?

2. Recall a time you intentionally refrained from purchasing or pursuing something even though you knew it would make you happy. What motivated your decision? Later, did you feel gratitude or regret about your decision? Why?

When God Doesn't Want Us Happy

3. Read aloud Matthew 6:31 – 33, 1 Peter 1:13 – 16; and 1 John 2:15 – 17, three passages that contrast the behaviors of believers and unbelievers.

   • Based on what you read, how would you characterize the primary differences between the two?

   • In what ways do you recognize these differences in our own culture, within your circle of friends, or in your own life?

> *St. Ignatius of Loyola notes that sin is unwillingness to trust that what God wants is our deepest happiness. Until I am absolutely convinced of this I will do everything I can to keep my hands on the controls of my life, because I think I know better than God what I need for my fulfillment.*
>
> DAVID G. BENNER
> *Surrender to Love*

> *When we want to be something other than the thing God wants us to be, we must be wanting what, in fact, will not make us happy.*
>
> C. S. LEWIS
> *The Problem of Pain*

4. To be holy means to be set apart for a noble use. In the New Testament, the Greek word for "holy," *hagios* [HAG-ee-os], is used not so much in reference to objects as it is in reference to people.[1]

   • What insights does the 1 Peter passage (from question 3) provide about what it means to be holy?

   • How does exercising self-control impact your happiness?

   • Do you think it is possible to pursue both holiness and happiness? Why or why not?

5. *The Message* offers a fresh perspective on the passage from 1 John:

   > Don't love the world's ways. Don't love the world's goods. Love of the world squeezes out love for the Father. Practically everything that goes on in the world — wanting your own way, wanting everything for yourself, wanting to appear important — has nothing to do with the Father. It just isolates you from him. The world and all its wanting, wanting, wanting is on the way out — but whoever does what God wants is set for eternity (1 John 2:15 – 17 MSG).

   • Refer back to your responses to the Individual Activity on page 62. To what degree, if any, might wanting your own way, wanting everything for yourself, or wanting to appear important be reflected in the desire you wrote down?

---

1. "Possessions, Treasure, Mammon, Wealth, Money," Johannes Eichler and Colin Brown, *New International Dictionary of New Testament Theology*, vol. 2, Colin Brown, gen. ed. (Grand Rapids: Zondervan, 1978, 1986), 829.

• When you consider the desire you identified on page 62, is it easy to classify it as either holy or worldly, or does it seem unclear to you? Based on the three passages in question 3, what biblical truths might help you to discern the difference?

God Wants Us to Be More than Happy

6. The Greek word for "blessed" means "more than happy." Read aloud the adapted verses below:

> *More than happy* are those who fear the LORD, who find great delight in his commands (Psalm 112:1).

> *More than happy* are those who keep his statutes and seek him with all their heart (Psalm 119:2).

> *More than happy* are the pure in heart, for they will see God (Matthew 5:8).

> *More than happy* is the one whose sin the Lord will never count against them (Romans 4:8).

How does reading the adapted verses impact your understanding of what it means to be blessed?

Everyone wants to be happy, to be blessed. Too many people are willfully refusing to pay attention to the one who wills our happiness and ignorantly supposing that the Christian way is a harder way to get what they want than doing it on their own. But they are wrong. God's ways and God's presence are where we experience the happiness that lasts. Do it the easy way.

EUGENE H. PETERSON
A Long Obedience in the Same Direction

7. The more we fall in love with God, the less attracted we will be to things that offer temporary happiness, and the greater our desire will be for the kind of happiness — blessedness — that only God can give. The psalmist writes:

> Take delight in the LORD, and he will give you the desires of your heart (Psalm 37:4).

cont.

How hopeful are you that this — an increased love of God and diminished attraction to other things — is something you can experience in your relationship with God? Share the reasons for your response.

Individual Activity What I Want to Remember (2 Minutes)

Complete this activity on your own.

1. Briefly review the outline and any notes you took.

2. In the space below, write down the most significant thing you gained in this session — from the teaching, activities, or discussions.

   What I want to remember from this session ...

Closing Prayer

Close your time together with prayer.

✝ Between-Sessions Personal Study

● READ AND REFLECT

Read chapters 7, 8, and 9 of *The Christian Atheist*. Use the space below to note any insights or questions you want to bring to the next group session.

● HAPPILY BLESSED

Who doesn't want to be happy? Research tells us that happy people live longer, have better relationships, and are more satisfied with life. So happiness is good, right? Not so fast. The problem for us as Christian Atheists is not that we want to be happy but that we settle for happiness when God has so much more he wants to give us. God wants us to be more than happy — he wants us to be blessed.

> There is a formula that virtually no one would admit to, but if you look at the way we live you would have to admit that most of us believe this:
> better possessions + peaceful circumstances + thrilling experiences + the right relationships + the perfect appearance = happiness.
>
> *The Christian Atheist* video

1. Take a moment to think back on some of the happiest moments of your life, from childhood to the present. Identify three or four events or experiences and write them briefly in the space provided. For each happy moment, indicate which components of the happiness formula contributed to your experience of happiness. For example, right relationships and perfect appearance may have contributed to the happiness of a wedding day.

   Happy moment 1:

   ☐ Better possessions
   ☐ Peaceful circumstances
   ☐ Thrilling experiences
   ☐ Right relationships
   ☐ Perfect appearance

   Happy moment 2:

   ☐ Better possessions
   ☐ Peaceful circumstances
   ☐ Thrilling experiences
   ☐ Right relationships
   ☐ Perfect appearance

   Happy moment 3:

   ☐ Better possessions
   ☐ Peaceful circumstances
   ☐ Thrilling experiences
   ☐ Right relationships
   ☐ Perfect appearance

   Happy moment 4:

   ☐ Better possessions
   ☐ Peaceful circumstances
   ☐ Thrilling experiences
   ☐ Right relationships
   ☐ Perfect appearance

- What component shows up most in your happy moments? Which shows up least?

- Are there any happy moments for which you checked all the boxes or none of the boxes? What is particularly unique about that moment?

- Overall, what insights do the boxes you checked — or did not check — provide about what makes you happy?

We are not happy with the things of this world because we're not made for this world!... Earth is not heaven. It was never meant to be. That's why no amount of money, new house, new living-room furniture, new kitchen appliances, new clothes, new hair, new baby, new vacation, new job, new income, new husband, or new *anything* will ever satisfy us, because we were not made for the things of this world.

The Christian Atheist, page 173

2. When Jesus referred to the things of this world, he meant anything and everything that might distract us or draw our hearts away from God. The world is not neutral; it is a force so strong and so opposed to God that it renders us incapable of loving him.

> Do not love this world nor the things it offers you, for when you love the world, you do not have the love of the Father in you. For the world offers only a craving for physical pleasure, a craving for everything we see, and pride in our achievements and possessions. These are not from the Father, but are from this world. And this world is fading away, along with everything that people crave. But anyone who does what pleases God will live forever (1 John 2:15 – 17 NLT).

The passage focuses on three desires or cravings that turn our hearts away from God: sensuality, materialism, and conceit.

Sensuality ("physical pleasure"): excessive indulgence in sensual pleasures. Sensuality includes all five senses: sight, hearing, smell, touch, and taste. Which of the five senses represents the desire or craving you're most likely to indulge in (for example: taste might represent a craving for food or overeating)?

Materialism ("everything we see"): preoccupation with material objects and comforts. What objects or comforts occupy your thinking or routinely make withdrawals from your bank account (for example: shoes or clothing, electronics, spa treatments, etc.)?

Conceit ("pride in achievements and possessions"): an excessively favorable opinion of one's own ability or importance. In what ways do you engage in image management or try to prop up your significance in order to make yourself appear to be better or more than you are?

The passage contrasts temporary pleasures and self-serving desires with the eternal rewards of loving and serving God. What do you think makes it especially hard for you to love God and to choose him over the things you wrote down — your sensuality, materialism, and conceit?

The more you fall in love with God, the less the things of this world will pull you and draw you. You sincerely desire more than anything else to live a life that doesn't bring you temporary happiness.

The Christian Atheist video

3. In speaking about what it means to love and serve God, Jesus referred to our treasures and the importance of putting God first.

> Don't store up treasures here on earth, where moths eat them and rust destroys them, and where thieves break in and steal. Store your treasures in heaven, where moths and rust cannot destroy, and thieves do not break in and steal. Wherever your treasure is, there the desires of your heart will also be (Matthew 6:19 – 21 NLT).

> So don't worry about these things, saying, "What will we eat? What will we drink? What will we wear?" These things dominate the thoughts of unbelievers, but your heavenly Father already knows all your needs. Seek the Kingdom of God above all else, and live righteously, and he will give you everything you need (Matthew 6:31 – 33 NLT).

The Greek word used for "treasures" refers to a place where something is kept — a treasure box, chest, or storeroom.[2] As a metaphor for the human heart, it evokes the image of a secure container used to protect what matters most to us. In *The Divine Conspiracy*, author and pastor Dallas Willard notes what this means for our relationship with God:

> The most important commandment of the Judeo-Christian tradition is to treasure God and his realm more than anything else. That is what it means to love God with all your heart, soul, mind, and strength. It means to *treasure* him.

Based on the Matthew passages, how would you describe the difference between enjoying something as a gift from God and treasuring something? For example, what distinctions, if any, would you

---

2. "Holiness, Holy," Emmet Russell, *The New International Dictionary of the Bible*, Merrill C. Tenney, gen. ed. (Grand Rapids: Zondervan, 1987), 445.

make between merely enjoying food or clothing and treasuring those things?

When we treasure something, we place great value on it. We want to protect it and care for it. How does the idea of treasuring help you understand what it means for you to love God?

God wants so much more for you than mere happiness. Are you able to believe it, deep-down-in-your-gut believe it? He wants to bless you and give you joy — a deep joy the Bible says will fill you up to overflowing, put your feet to dancing, and make you want to shout and sing. That's a lot of joy! Why settle for second-class trinkets when God offers you a first-class ticket to so much more — boundless love, joy to the brim, peace beyond understanding, and eternity with him.

When You Believe in God but Don't Want to Go Overboard

LUKEWARM
[look-wawrm]
just slightly warm, especially when expected to be hot; having little ardor, zeal, or enthusiasm; indifferent; apathetic

VOMIT
[**vom**-it]
to eject violently by mouth; spew forth; aka barf or hurl

SURRENDER
[*suh*-**ren**-der]
to yield to the possession or power of another; admit defeat; relinquish

EVERYTHING
[**ev**-ree-thing]
every element of an aggregate; all; the lot; total; whole

OVERBOARD
[**oh**-ver-bawrd, -bohrd]
to go to extremes

Group Discussion Checking In (5 Minutes)

Welcome to session 6 of *The Christian Atheist*. A key part of getting to know God better is sharing your journey with each other. Before watching the video, briefly check in with each other about your experiences since the last session. For example:

- What insights did you discover in the personal study or in the chapters you read from *The Christian Atheist* book?
- How did the last session impact your daily life or your relationship with God?
- What questions would you like to ask the other members of your group?

Video When You Believe in God but Don't Want to Go Overboard (18 Minutes)

Play the video segment for session 6. As you watch, use the outline below to follow along or to take notes on anything that stands out to you.

Notes

Many so-called Christians are lukewarm. They want enough of Jesus to get them by, but not so much that they go overboard.

"I know your deeds, that you are neither cold nor hot. I wish you were either one or the other! So, because you are lukewarm — neither hot nor cold — I am about to spit you out of my mouth" (Revelation 3:15 – 16).

Lukewarm Christians …
1. Crave acceptance from people more than acceptance from God.
2. Rarely share their faith in Christ.
3. Do whatever it takes to alleviate their guilt.
4. Think more about life on earth than eternity in heaven.
5. Gauge their morality by comparing themselves to others.
6. Want to be saved from the penalty of sin without changing their lives.
7. Only turn to God when they're in a bind or when they're in trouble.
8. Give when it doesn't impinge on their standard of living.
9. Are not much different from the rest of this world.
10. Want the benefits of what Christ did without conforming to who he is.

When we put God on the shelf and say, "I believe in you, but I don't really need you right now," Jesus says, very clearly, that makes God want to puke.

If we're not overboard for him, then chances are we don't really know him.

It's time to seek him. It's time to surrender everything. It's time to let go of everything in this world.

"Here I am! I stand at the door and knock. If anyone hears my voice and opens the door, I will come in and eat with that person, and they with me" (Revelation 3:20).

Group Discussion | **When You Believe in God but Don't Want to Go Overboard** (5 Minutes)

Take a few minutes to talk about what you just watched.

1. What part of the teaching had the most impact on you?

2. What do you imagine people have in mind when they think something like, "I believe in God, but I don't want to go overboard"?

Individual Activity | **Temperature Check** (5 Minutes)

Complete this activity on your own.

1. Briefly review the ten characteristics of lukewarm Christians on page 75. Circle the one characteristic you relate to most — the one that is or once was a struggle for you. Write it in the space below.

2. How would you describe the degree to which you struggle with this characteristic?

  ☐ It's rarely a struggle for me.
  ☐ It's occasionally a struggle for me.
  ☐ It's sometimes a struggle for me.
  ☐ It's frequently a struggle for me.
  ☐ It's nearly always a struggle for me.

3. If possible, recall your most recent experience of this characteristic. In the moment, to what degree were you aware that you might be compromising your faith depending on how you responded?

☐ I was unaware of it in the moment.
☐ I was slightly aware of it in the moment.
☐ I was moderately aware of it in the moment.
☐ I was mostly aware of it in the moment.
☐ I was highly aware of it in the moment.

4. Overall, how would you describe your spiritual temperature? Place an X on the continuum below to indicate your response.

Stone Cold   Lukewarm   White Hot

Group Discussion (25 Minutes)

Temperature Check

1. In what ways does the characteristic you identified in the Individual Activity typically show up in your life (for example: in your decisions, relationships, lifestyle choices, etc.)? If you feel comfortable doing so, share an example of a recent or past experience to illustrate your response.

2. How do you feel about your spiritual temperature?

> The terrible thing, the almost impossible thing, is to hand over your whole self—all your wishes and precautions—to Christ. But it is far easier than what we are trying to do instead. For what we are trying to do is to remain what we call "ourselves," to keep personal happiness as our great aim in life, and yet at the same time be "good." We are all trying to let our mind and heart go their own way—centered on money or pleasure or ambition—and hoping, in spite of this, to behave honestly and chastely and humbly. And that is exactly what Christ warned us you could not do.
>
> C. S. LEWIS
> *Mere Christianity*

Lukewarm Christians

3. Of the ten characteristics of lukewarm Christians listed on page 75, what two or three would you say are most common among Christians you know? Why do you think so many followers of Jesus struggle with these two or three issues especially?

4. The church in Laodicea described in Revelation 3 is the prototype of lukewarm Christianity. Read the passage below aloud.

> I know all the things you do, that you are neither hot nor cold. I wish that you were one or the other! But since you are like lukewarm water, neither hot nor cold, I will spit you out of my mouth! You say, "I am rich. I have everything I want. I don't need a thing!" And you don't realize that you are wretched and miserable and poor and blind and naked. So I advise you to buy gold from me — gold that has been purified by fire. Then you will be rich. Also buy white garments from me so you will not be shamed by your nakedness, and ointment for your eyes so you will be able to see. I correct and discipline everyone I love. So be diligent and turn from your indifference (Revelation 3:15 – 19 NLT).

What would you say is the Laodiceans' root sin — the primary failure that ultimately led them to become lukewarm toward God? For example, would you say it was pride, self-reliance, materialism, misplaced trust? In what ways do you recognize this same root sin among Christians in your community or in yourself?

The Laodiceans were self-deceived about their true spiritual condition. According to the passage, what is the remedy for their condition?

If you were to translate this remedy for Christians today, how would you describe it? What practical applications would you make?

Full-Time Christians

5. On the video, Craig said, "I realized I had become a full-time pastor and a part-time follower of Christ." In *Mere Christianity*, author C. S. Lewis writes about the problem with being a part-time Christian:

> Christ says "Give me All. I don't want so much of your time and so much of your money and so much of your work: I want You. I have not come to torment your natural self, but to kill it.... Hand over the whole natural self, all the desires which you think innocent as well as the ones you think wicked — the whole outfit. I will give you a new self instead. In fact, I will give you Myself: my own will shall become yours."

What stands out most to you from the quote?

Ninety-five percent devotion to Christ is 5 percent short.

BILL HYBELS

What folly to fear to be too entirely God's! It is to fear to be too happy.

FRANÇOIS FÉNELON
Christian Perfection

Jesus' followers are those who intentionally arrange their lives around the goal of spiritual transformation — the development of a well-ordered heart.

JOHN ORTBERG
The Life You've Always Wanted

What God gets out of our lives — and, indeed, what we get out of our lives — is simply the person we become.

DALLAS WILLARD
The Divine Conspiracy

How do you understand the difference between tormenting the natural self and killing it?

In what ways are you drawn to the idea of total surrender to Christ? What hopes does it stir in you?

Individual Activity What I Want to Remember (2 Minutes)

Complete this activity on your own.

1. Briefly review the outline and any notes you took.

2. In the space below, write down the most significant thing you gained in this session — from the teaching, activities, or discussions.

   What I want to remember from this session ...

Closing Prayer

Close your time together with prayer.

Final Personal Study

● READ AND REFLECT

Read the afterword of *The Christian Atheist*. Use the space below to note any insights or questions you have.

● WANTING MORE THAN ENOUGH OF JESUS

Christian Atheists have a lot in common with Goldilocks — we like things not too hot, not too cold, but just right. Yet when it comes to living out our faith, what might feel "just right" to us is what God considers nauseatingly lukewarm. God doesn't want a tepid commitment or a moderate devotion. He doesn't want us to settle for just-right or just-enough or a just-so life in Christ. He wants everything we've got — fierce commitment, wholehearted passion, and a blazing heart of love.

Many so-called Christians are lukewarm.... They want enough of Jesus to keep them out of hell and enough to get into heaven, but not so much of Jesus that he transforms their lives .... They want enough of Jesus to get them by, but not so much that they go overboard.

The Christian Atheist video

1. On the video, Craig describes ten characteristics of lukewarm Christians. For each of the following characteristics, circle the number that best describes your response.

(1) I crave acceptance from people more than acceptance from God.

Almost never true of me	Occasionally true of me	Sometimes true of me	Often true of me	Almost always true of me
1	2	3	4	5

(2) I rarely share my faith in Christ.

Almost never true of me	Occasionally true of me	Sometimes true of me	Often true of me	Almost always true of me
1	2	3	4	5

(3) I do whatever it takes to alleviate my guilt.

Almost never true of me	Occasionally true of me	Sometimes true of me	Often true of me	Almost always true of me
1	2	3	4	5

(4) I think more about life on earth than eternity in heaven.

Almost never true of me	Occasionally true of me	Sometimes true of me	Often true of me	Almost always true of me
1	2	3	4	5

(5) I gauge my morality by comparing myself to others (rather than Christ).

Almost never true of me	Occasionally true of me	Sometimes true of me	Often true of me	Almost always true of me
1	2	3	4	5

(6) I want to be saved from the penalty of sin without changing my life.

Almost never true of me	Occasionally true of me	Sometimes true of me	Often true of me	Almost always true of me
1	2	3	4	5

(7) I only turn to God when I'm in trouble.

Almost never true of me	Occasionally true of me	Sometimes true of me	Often true of me	Almost always true of me
1	2	3	4	5

(8) I give when it doesn't impinge on my standard of living.

| Almost never true of me | Occasionally true of me | Sometimes true of me | Often true of me | Almost always true of me |

(9) I am not much different from the rest of the world.

| Almost never true of me | Occasionally true of me | Sometimes true of me | Often true of me | Almost always true of me |

(10) I want the benefits of what Christ did without conforming to who he is.

| Almost never true of me | Occasionally true of me | Sometimes true of me | Often true of me | Almost always true of me |

Transfer your responses to the grid below. For example, if you circled 3 (Sometimes true of me) in response to the first question, place an X in the 3 column for question 1.

	1 ALMOST NEVER TRUE OF ME	2 OCCASIONALLY TRUE OF ME	3 SOMETIMES TRUE OF ME	4 OFTEN TRUE OF ME	5 ALMOST ALWAYS TRUE OF ME
1					
2					
3					
4					
5					
6					
7					
8					
9					
10					

Briefly review your summary chart on page 83. Based on your ten responses, how would you characterize your faith?

> Most wouldn't admit that this is all the faith they can manage. We want God's benefits without changing how we live. We want his best, without our sacrifices.
>
> *The Christian Atheist*, page 236

2. Of the Christians in ancient Crete the apostle Paul wrote: "They claim to know God, but by their actions they deny him. They are detestable, disobedient and unfit for doing anything good" (Titus 1:16). Paul's letter to the preacher Titus addressed this problem in the church and emphasized the vital connection between belief and practice:

   > For the grace of God has been revealed, bringing salvation to all people. And we are instructed to turn from godless living and sinful pleasures. We should live in this evil world with wisdom, righteousness, and devotion to God, while we look forward with hope to that wonderful day when the glory of our great God and Savior, Jesus Christ, will be revealed. He gave his life to free us from every kind of sin, to cleanse us, and to make us his very own people, totally committed to doing good deeds (Titus 2:11 – 14 NLT).

   According to the passage, what motives do we have for living a life of devotion to God?

   Would you describe them as negative motives (based on fear) or positive motives (based on good things)?

Read the passage once more, this time in *The Message*:

God's readiness to give and forgive is now public. Salvation's available for everyone! We're being shown how to turn our backs on a godless, indulgent life, and how to take on a God-filled, God-honoring life. This new life is starting right now, and is whetting our appetites for the glorious day when our great God and Savior, Jesus Christ, appears. He offered himself as a sacrifice to free us from a dark, rebellious life into this good, pure life, making us a people he can be proud of, energetic in goodness (Titus 2:11 – 14 MSG).

Several words and phrases in the passage describe the characteristics of the new life God calls us to. For each of the following characteristics, consider the promise or hope that word or phrase represents for you. Why would you want this to be a characteristic that authentically describes you?

God-filled

God-honoring

Good

Pure

A [person] he can be proud of

Energetic in goodness

"Whatever it takes" became my heart's cry. Whatever it takes to know him. Whatever it takes to live like I truly love God. Whatever it takes to love eternity more than this world. Even if I have to fight, scrape, and crawl away from my Christian Atheism into a genuine, crucified life of faith and radical obedience to Christ, I'll do whatever it takes.

The Christian Atheist, page 235

3. Where would you say you are right now? Place an X on the continuum to indicate your response.

I am not yet ready to make changes in my life.	I am ready to do whatever it takes to live like I truly love God.

Wherever you placed yourself on the continuum, take a few moments to talk with God about it. Express your heart to God — tell him how you feel about your relationship. Ask him for what you need — strength, forgiveness, wisdom, healing, deliverance. Then spend a few moments listening for anything God might want to say to you in response. Close your time by thanking God for his love and his goodness to you. If you wish, use the space below to write your prayer or to note anything you want to remember.

Wholly surrendered. Those are beautiful, nourishing words for a God-hungry heart. They mark the beginning of a journey from life as it is to life as it could be. A life of knowing God and allowing yourself to be known by him. Of walking through hardships and loss steady in the hope that God is out to do you only good. Of experiencing the deep love of Christ every day. Of discovering God's trustworthy provision when you put him in charge of your money and your happiness. These are the kinds of things that lead to the life that is truly life. And isn't that what you really want? If so, it's time to jump ship from Christian Atheism and go completely overboard — take a flying leap of white-hot faith and let the God who loves you catch you.

Welcome to true Christianity.

The Christian Atheist

Believing in God but Living as If He Doesn't Exist

Craig Groeschel

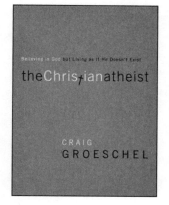

"The more I looked, the more I found Christian Atheists everywhere."

Former Christian Atheist Craig Groeschel knows his subject all too well. After over a decade of successful ministry, he had to make a painful self admission: although he believed in God, he was leading his church like God didn't exist.

To Christians and non-Christians alike, to the churched and the unchurched, the journey leading up to Groeschel's admission and the journey that follows—from his family and his upbringing to the lackluster and even diametrically opposed expressions of faith he encountered—will look and sound like the story of their own lives.

Now the founding and senior pastor of the multicampus, pace-setting LifeChurch.tv, Groeschel's personal journey toward a more authentic God-honoring life is more relevant than ever.

Available in stores and online!

Weird

Because Normal Isn't Working

Craig Groeschel,
author of The Christian Atheist

Normal people are stressed, overwhelmed, and exhausted. Many of their relationships are, at best, strained and, in most cases, just surviving. Even though we live in one of the most prosperous places on earth, normal is still living paycheck to paycheck and never getting ahead. In our oversexed world, lust, premarital sex, guilt, and shame are far more common than purity, virginity, and a healthy married sex life. And when it comes to God, the majority believe in him, but the teachings of Scripture rarely make it into their everyday lives.

Simply put, normal isn't working.

Groeschel's WEIRD views will help you break free from the norm to lead a radically abnormal (and endlessly more fulfilling) life. Available as a hardcover book and as a DVD-based curriculum for small groups. A study guide is also available for use with the DVD.

Available in stores and online!

It Hardcover Book and It Book/DVD Bundle

How Churches and Leaders Can Get It and Keep It

Craig Groeschel

When Craig Groeschel founded LifeChurch.tv, the congregation met in a borrowed two-car garage, with ratty furnishings and faulty audiovisual equipment. But people were drawn there, sensing a powerful, life-changing force Groeschel calls "IT." Based on the bestselling book of the same name, the nine-session It video journey helps users discover the powerful presence from God that Groeschel calls IT at work in many churches. Each video session is approximately ten minutes long and focuses on the many facets of "what is IT and where did IT come from?" Groeschel will explore the necessary contributions to IT, such as vision, divine focus, unmistakable camaraderie, innovative minds, willingness to fall short, hearts focused outward, and kingdom-mindedness. The video experience concludes with a session on "do you have IT and how to keep IT once you have IT." The video is designed for leadership groups and church groups and includes discussion questions on the DVD at the end of each session.